GORILL K
G000254637
by Anne Wright
ὁ γοριλλος ἐστι...
The Gorilla is...

Can you discover what the Gorilla is?

First, you need to **decipher** the letters in the caption. They are all written in Classical Greek letters, but you will see that some letters look like English letters (for example, ε = e).

However, some letters are rather different and you will need to use the guide to the Greek alphabet at the back of this book to work out what they mean. For example, λ = l, while ρ represents an r, not a p.

Next you need to **work out** what the caption means. An enormous number of English words come from Greek and each page gives an English word to help you. For example, a *micro**scope*** is used to look at *small* things. The micro– part of the English word means small.

Once you have decided what the caption means, you can **check** your code-cracking skills by looking at the words which are printed upside down. They tell you what the Greek sentence means.

You can also look up the meaning of Greek words in the mini-dictionary at the end of the book.

Good luck!

ὁ γοριλλος ἐστι μικρος.

The Gorilla is small.

English word: <u>micro</u>scope

ὁ γοριλλος ἐστι θερμος.

The Gorilla is hot.

English word: <u>thermo</u>meter

ὁ γοριλλος ἐστι φιλιος.
The Gorilla is friendly.
English word: <u>phil</u>osopher
(= lover of wisdom)

ὁ γοριλλος
ἐστι μαθητης.
The Gorilla is a student.
English word: <u>math</u>ematics (literally:
'things learned')

ὁ γοριλλος ἐστι κριτης.
The Gorilla is a judge.
English words: critic; critical

Greek Around You 1 — Maths

The Greeks made many important discoveries in mathematics. Indeed, the word **mathematics** is a Greek word – μαθηματικα or 'things learned'. Several branches of maths are also Greek in origin. **Arithmetic** comes from ἀριθμος ('a number'), while **geometry** literally means 'measuring the earth' and comes from γη ('earth') and μετρια ('measurement').

Can you work out the names of these shapes or things? Note that δια = 'across', συμ = 'together' and μετρος = 'a measure'.

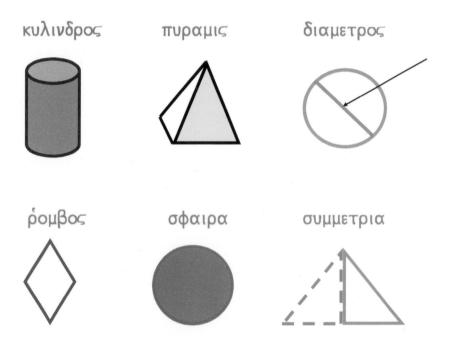

κυλινδρος

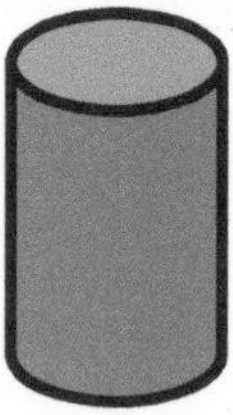

πυραμις

διαμετρος

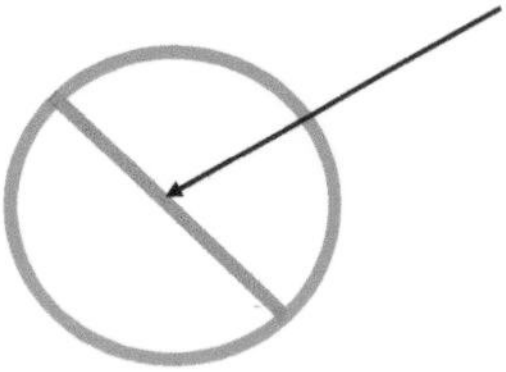

ῥομβος

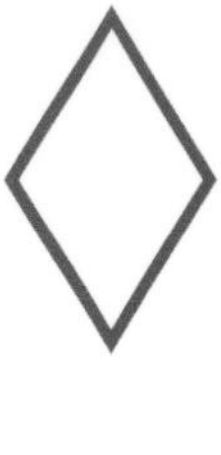

σφαιρα

συμμετρια

Answers: cylinder, pyramid, diameter, rhombus, sphere, symmetry

Some mathematical words are a little more complicated. For example, an **isosceles** triangle has two equal sides. The Greek word ἰσοσκελης means ‘with equal legs’. Similarly, a **trapezoid** (τραπεζοειδη) literally means ‘table-like’ (τραπεζα means ‘a table’). Finally, a **parallelogram** (παραλληλογραμμος) means ‘bounded by parallel lines’.

ἰσοσκελης τραπεζοειδη παραλληλογραμμος

Mathematicians also use Greek to explain how many sides a shape has. For example, ἑξ means ‘six’ and γωνια means ‘angle’, so a **hexagon** has six sides. Similarly, πολυ means ‘many’, so a **polygon** has many sides. ἑδρα means ‘base’, so a **polyhedron** has many faces.

shape	**Greek**	**meaning of Greek**
pentagon	πεντε	5
hexagon	ἑξ	6
heptagon	ἑπτα	7
octagon	ὀκτω	8
decahedron	δεκα	10
dodecahedron	δωδεκα	12

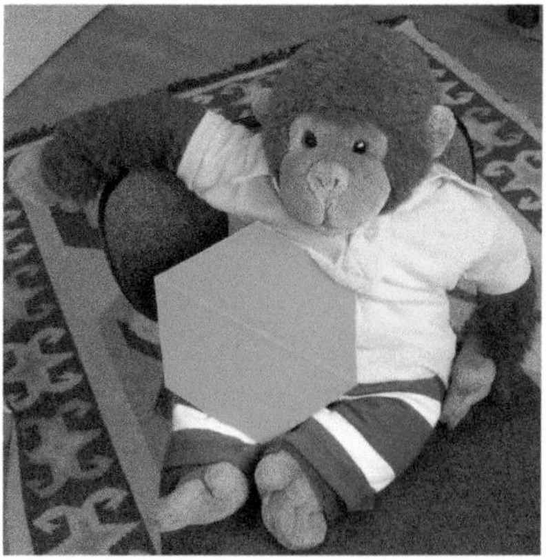

The name nonagon (nine-sided shape) comes partly from Latin.

ὁ γοριλλος
ἐστι μουσικος.
The Gorilla is musical.
English word: music

ὁ γοριλλος ἐστι σοφος.

The Gorilla is clever.

English word: <u>soph</u>isticated

(=knowledgeable, smart)

ὁ γοριλλος
ἐστιν ἀρχαιολογικος.
The Gorilla is an archaeologist (literally: knowledgeable about ancient things).
English word: archaeology

ὁ γοριλλος ἐστι
τεχνικος.
The Gorilla is artistic.
English word: technical

The Greeks greatly enjoyed art and music. There were nine goddesses (known as **Muses** — Μουσαι) who were thought to look after cultural pursuits. The Muses gave their name to **music** (μουσικη) and **museum** (μουσειον). Even now, a poet may refer to their **Muse** (someone who inspires them).

In art, any word which has **–graph** or **tech–** in it comes from Greek. **–graph** comes from the Greek γραφω, 'I write' or 'I draw', and **tech–** comes from τεχνη, 'skill'. For example, both **graphics** (a visual presentation) and **technique** (skill) come from Greek.

English also uses more complicated words. **Photograph** comes from φως ('light') and γραφω, and is an image created by light striking a light-sensitive surface. **Lithograph** is a compound of λιθος ('stone') and γραφω, and is a printing process where a drawing is etched into stone. **Technology** comes from τεχνη and λογος ('word'), but is used to mean knowledge of a variety of tools, not just skill with words.

Some names in art still mean the same thing that they did 2,500 years ago. **Cyan** (κυανος) is still blue, while **sepia** (σηπια) got its name from the cuttlefish, which spurts out an inky dye to confuse predators. Similarly, an **architect** (ἀρχιτεχτων) still designs buildings and **ceramics** (κεραμεικος) still means working with clay. In fact, one area of Athens had so many potters working in it that it became known as the Κεραμεικος, or 'Potters' Quarters'.

While many terms in music come from Italian, a number come from Greek, although their meaning may have changed over time. For example, an ὀρχηστρα originally meant the area where a χορος danced in the θεατρον, but has come to mean a large group of instrumentalists playing together.

A number of musical terms use the Greek word φωνη ('voice'). For example, a **xylophone** is made of wood (ξυλον) and συμφωνια literally means 'voices together' (συμ = 'together'). If an orchestra did not play together it would make a κακοφωνια (κακος = 'bad') and would not be in ἁρμονια ('agreement').

Can you work out these other musical terms?
Two or more notes played together: χωρδη
Some composers write variations on an original θεμα
The beat of a piece: ῥυθμος
Kettledrums: τυμπανα
You often use this to pluck a guitar: πληκτρον
Like a small guitar: λυρα
Churchgoers may sing these: ψαλμος, ὑμνος

Answers:
orchestra, chorus, theatre

symphony, cacophony, harmony

chord, theme, rhythm, timpani,
plectrum, lyre, psalm, hymn

ὁ γοριλλος ἐστιν ἀρχιτεκτων.
The Gorilla is an architect.
English word: <u>architecture</u>

ὁ γοριλλος ἐστι στρατιωτης.

The Gorilla is a soldier.

English word: <u>strat</u>egic

ὁ γοριλλος ἐστι ποιητης.

Gorillas are amazing,
Gorillas are smart.
Gorillas are Great Apes.
Great Apes are Great Art.

The Gorilla is a poet.

English word: poetical

ὁ γοριλλος ἐστι
ναυτης.
The Gorilla is a sailor.
English word: nautical

Lots of more advanced vocabulary in English comes from Greek. For example, an **emporium** is a word for a large shop and comes from ἐμποριον, the Greek for a trading-place. (One Greek colony in Spain was even called Ἐμποριον.)

However, lots of technical words in English also come from Greek. For example, a **glossary** provides a list of important technical words used in a book. It comes from γλωσσαριον - a 'small word' or a 'foreign word'. A **pseudonym** is a pen-name used by an author who does not want to use their real name. The English word is derived from two Greek words, ψευδης ('false') and ὀνομα ('name'). An **anonymous** writer (ἀν - 'without' and ὀνομα - 'name') avoids using their name at all. Again, the word is a compound of two Greek words. Finally, a **synonym** (συν - 'together', ὀνομα - 'name') is a word which has the same meaning as another.

The original meanings of words which we use regularly in English can sometimes be quite unusual. For example, an **anthology** is used to refer to a collection of poetry or prose. However, the Greek word ἀνθολογια literally means 'flower-gathering'. This is because an anthology was a short collection of poems put together like a posy of flowers. The name for an **encyclopaedia** comes from three Greek words: ἐν ('in'), κυκλος ('a circle') and παιδεια ('education'). However, the Greek phrase meant 'general education' rather than a detailed reference work.

Many words which describe literary techniques come from Greek. An author who uses **pathos** (παθος - 'suffering') aims to rouse the reader's **sympathy** (συν - 'together', παθος - 'suffering') for a **character** (χαρακτηρ). People use **sarcasm** to say the opposite of what they really mean ('You're so clever, aren't you?'). Sarcasm comes from the Greek word σαρκαζω - 'to tear flesh'. **Irony** is similar to sarcasm and comes from the Greek εἰρωνεια - 'pretended ignorance'.

Can you work out what the following words mean?

κομμα ποιημα παραγραφη κολον ἀποστροφη

θεσαυρος συλλαβη μεταφορα ποιητης

Answers (including some literal meanings of the Greek words):

comma—'a short clause'

poem — 'a thing done'

paragraph—'a thing written beside' (παρα = 'beside'; γραφω = 'I write')

colon—'broken off' or 'stunted'

apostrophe—'twisting away'

thesaurus— 'treasure' or 'treasury'

syllable—'that which is held together'

metaphor — transferring the meaning from one word to another (μετα = 'over', 'across'; φερω = 'I carry')

poet —'a maker'

some names come from Greek...
ὁ γοριλλος ἀνδρειος ἐστιν.
The Gorilla is brave.
names: Andrew (= brave); Andrea

ὁ γοριλλος ἐχει
δωρον.
The Gorilla has a gift.
names: Dorothy; Theodore
(gift of god)

ὁ γοριλλος ἐστι
βασιλευς
The Gorilla is a king.
names: Basil (= regal); Vassily

ὁ γοριλλος ἐστι
καλος.
The Gorilla is handsome.
name: Callista (= very beautiful)

Lots of English names originally come from saints' names in the Christian Bible (from βιβλος— a book). The New Testament was written in Greek because Greek was widely spoken around the Mediterranean. This means that many technical terms in Christianity come from Greek. Indeed, the word Christ means 'The Anointed One', and comes from the Greek χριστος, or oil to be smeared on the body. Similarly, the Apostles took their title from their job. They were sent out to preach and ἀποστελλω means 'I send forth'.

Sometimes, religious words reflect historical dangers. For example, a crypt is a burial place beneath a church. The word comes from κρυπτω, 'I hide' and reflects the fact that for a long time Christianity was forbidden in Greece and Rome, so Christians had to bury their dead in secret places. Similarly, a martyr suffers for their beliefs and the word comes from the Greek μαρτυρος, or 'witness'. This is because many early Christians suffered when they gave witness to their faith.

Some words had an original Christian meaning, but have acquired a wider meaning. For example, angel comes from ἀγγελος - 'a messenger'. An evangelist literally means someone who announces good news and is a compound of εὐ ('well') and ἀγγελος. Nowadays, an evangelist can mean a preacher for any cause, as well as a historical preacher, such as St Luke. Orthodox means holding established beliefs and comes from the Greek ὀρθος 'right' and δοξα 'opinion'. The opposite is heterodox, or holding alternate (ἑτερος) views.

Theology is the study of religion (θεος - 'god' and λογος - 'word'). Other English terms are also derived from θεος. An atheist does not believe in god (ἀ- 'without'), while many of the world's major religions are monotheist (μονος - 'sole', 'alone'). For example, followers of Islam believe in only one god. In contrast, the Greeks were polytheists and believed in lots of gods (πολυ - 'many').

The Greeks were also very interested in philosophy, or the pursuit of wisdom (literally φιλος 'love' of σοφια 'wisdom'). Philosophy included λογικη or logic (reasoning) and ἤθικα or ethics (right and wrong). Philosophy also tried to explain the nature of being (or what things are). This has come to be called metaphysics - μεταφυσικα. Although the most famous Greek philosophers are Socrates (Σωκρατης), Plato (Πλατων) and Aristotle (᾿Αριστοτελης), there were many others. Thales (Θαλης) was the first philosopher to try to explain the world without referring to the gods and Democritus (Δημοκριτος) suggested that everything was made up of atoms.

What do we get from...?

ἀρχαγγελος
μοναστεριον
καθεδρα
βλασφημια

Answers:
archangel
monastery
cathedral
blasphemy (speaking evil)

Greek has a number of little words which show where something is. For example, ἐν means 'in' or 'on' and ὑπο can mean 'under'. Can you work out where the Gorilla is?

ὁ γοριλλος ἐστιν ἐν τῃ γῇ.

The Gorilla is on the ground.

English word: geography

ὁ γοριλλος ἐστιν
ἐν τῃ οἰκιᾳ.
The Gorilla is in the house.
English word: <u>ec</u>onomics
(literally: ‘the laws of the house’)

ὁ γοριλλος ἐστιν ἐν τῳ Μουσειῳ.

The Gorilla is in the Museum.

English word: museum

ὁ γοριλλος ἐστιν ὑπο τῳ ἡλιῳ.

The Gorilla is under the sun.

English words: <u>Helios</u> (sun-god); <u>heli</u>um

Greek Around You 5 Geography

The word geography comes from two Greek words—**γη** ('land') and **γραφω** ('I write'). Some countries or regions also take their name from Greek. **Can you work out what the following names are?**

Λυβυη 'Ιταλια **Εὐρωπη** 'Ασια

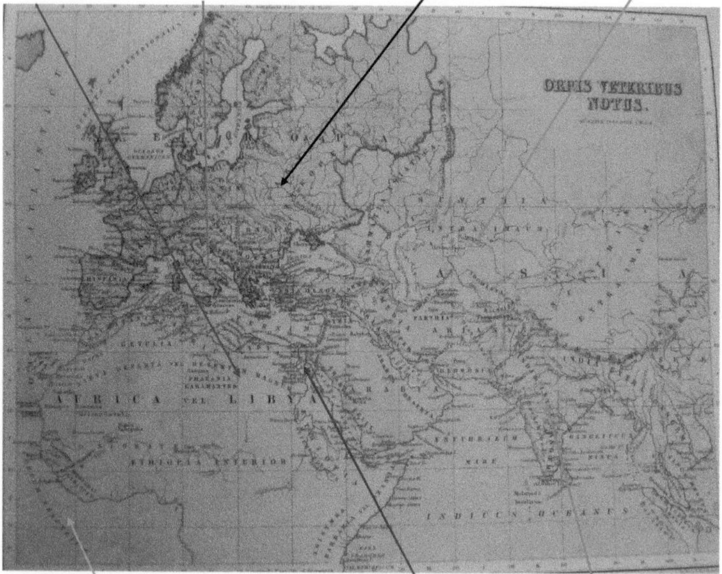

ὠκεανος 'Ατλαντικος **Αἰγυπτος** 'Ινδια

The Greeks borrowed the name for India from Sanskrit (an ancient Indian language). However, some regions take their name from mythology. Atlas (**'Ατλας**) was a giant who held up the world on his shoulders and was then turned into stone. Mount Atlas was in North Africa, so the ocean which lies off North Africa was called the Atlantic Ocean.

Answers: Lybia, Italy, Europe, Asia, Atlantic Ocean, Egypt, India

Other names are slightly less obvious. The Arctic takes its name from ἀρκτικος, which literally means 'near the Bear'. The Bear is a northern constellation, so the region has been called after the star. (Antarctic comes from ἀντι— 'opposite' and ἀρκτικος.) Australia and New Zealand are sometimes called the Antipodes. This literally means 'with feet opposite' (ἀντι and ποδες— 'feet') and reflected the fact that early explorers thought of these islands as being on the other side of the globe.

Lots of technical terms in geography also come from Greek. The Nile delta takes its name from an upside-down capital Δ, since the Nile spreads out in this shape as it reaches the coast. A cyclone comes from the Greek verb κυκλοω, which means 'to circle' and, although the Greeks did not know that earthquakes were caused by shifting tectonic plates, the Greek word τεκτονικος ('relating to building') is used to describe them.

Some Greek words have identical meanings today. For example, the mouth of a volcano is still called a κρατηρ. Other words are spelled slightly differently. **Do you know what these mean?**

χασμα, ἰσθμος, ἐκλειψις and καταρακτος

Answers:
chasm—yawning hollow
isthmus—neck of land between two seas
eclipse—when the moon or sun disappears
cataract—powerful waterfall

Verbs

In Greek, the ending of a verb changes to tell you who is doing an action. So far you have read lots of sentences with the verb ἐστι - 'he is' or 'is' (sometimes ἐστιν). To say 'I am' or 'you are', Greek uses a different form of this verb. εἰμι = I am and εἰ = you are.

γοριλλος εἰ
πανθηρ εἰ

Greek also has plural forms of the verb. These are used when more than one person is involved.

ἐσμεν = we are   ἐστε = you are   εἰσι or εἰσιν = they are

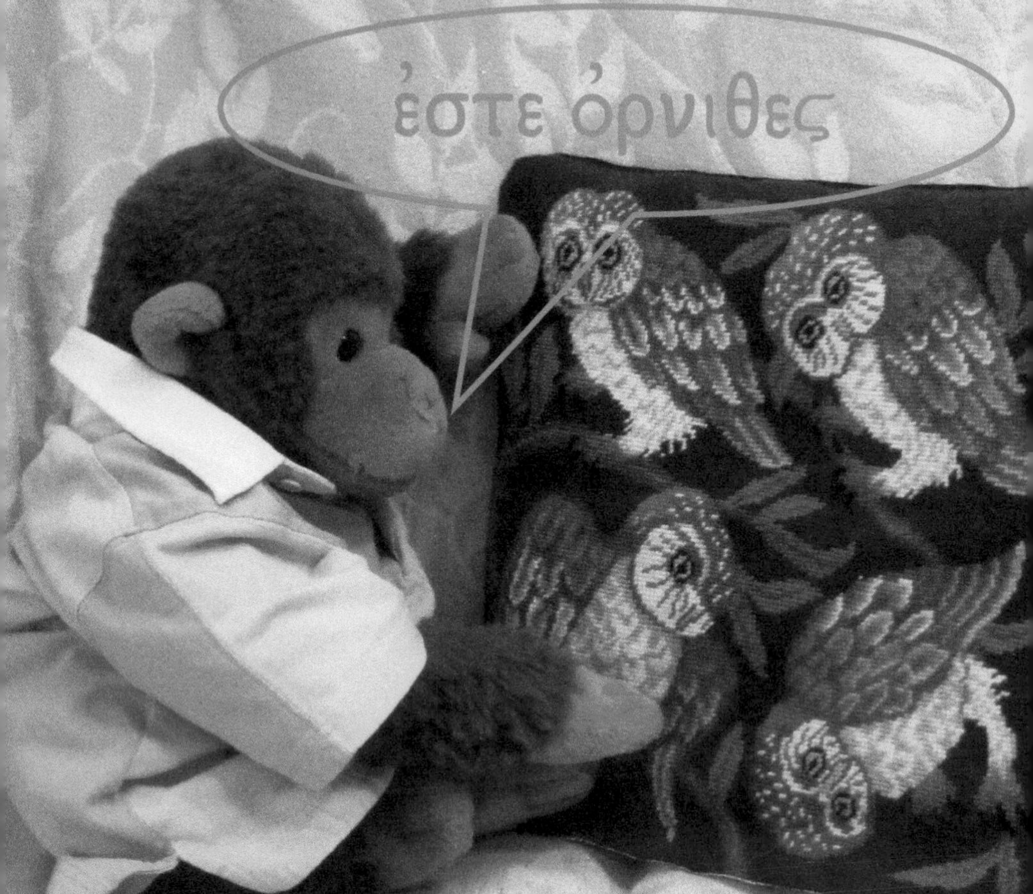

You are birds.

English word: <u>ornith</u>ology

ὁ γοριλλος και ὁ
παρδαλις εἰσι φιλοι.
ἐσμεν φιλοι
The Gorilla and the Leopard are
friends. (φιλοι is the plural of φιλος)
English word: leo<u>pard</u>

Greek Around You 6 Science (1)

Lots of scientific words come from Greek. In particular, the names of many branches of science end in –**onomy** or –**ology**. This is because **νομος** is the Greek for 'law' and **λογος** is the Greek for 'word' or 'calculation'. For example, **astronomy** (**ἀστηρ** + **νομος**) literally means studying the 'law of the stars'. **Geology** (**γη** + **λογος**) means 'calculating the land' (or the study of the rocks which make up Earth).

The first six subjects are fairly obvious, but can you find out what someone studying the other subjects would learn?

Science	**Greek word(s)**	**meaning of Greek**
Biology	βιος	life
Microbiology	μικρος, βιος	small, life
Zoology	ζῷον	animal
Ornithology	ὀρνιθες	birds
Anthropology	ἀνθρωπος	man
Seismology	σεισμος	earthquake
Meteorology	μετεωρος	high in the air
Pharmacology	φαρμακον	poison, drug
Ecology	οἰκος	house, animal's lair
Genealogy	γενος	race
Cosmology	κοσμος	universe
Psychology	ψυχη	soul

Answers: the study of the weather; how medical drugs work; the environment; tracing your ancestors; the origins of the universe; the science of the mind.

Some scientific instruments also take their name from Greek. In particular, instruments of measurement often end in –**meter** (from **μετρον** – 'a measurement'). For example, **βαρος** means weight and a **barometer** measures atmospheric pressure (or air pressure). Similarly, an instrument which is used to look at something often end in –**scope**, from the Greek **σκοπει** ('it looks').

What are instruments which investigate the following called?

Greek	**meaning**
θερμος	heat
ἀνεμος	wind
χρονος	time
μικρος	small
τελος	far
στηθος	chest

Answers: thermometer, anemometer, chronometer, microscope, telescope, stethoscope.

Not all branches of science end in –onomy or –ology. For example, **physics** (the properties of matter and energy) comes from the Greek **φυσικα**, or 'natural things'.

Verbs

The verb for 'I am' is quite an unusual verb. Most Greek verbs follow an easy pattern. The **start** of the verb shows the basic meaning and the **endings** show who is doing the action.

For example, γραφω means 'I write'. The γραφ– bit gives the basic meaning 'write', while the –ω ending shows that 'I' am doing the writing.

Similarly, γραφει means 'he' or 'she' writes. The γραφ– bit gives the basic meaning 'write', while the –ει ending shows that '**he**' or '**she**' is doing the writing.

If we were to write out all the different forms of the verb we would see that it went:

γραφω	I write
γραφεις	**you** write
γραφει	**he** or **she** writes
γραφομεν	**we** write
γραφετε	**you** write
γραφουσι	**they** write (γραφουσιν at the end of a sentence)

Why are there two forms of 'you'? γραφεις is used when there is only one person and γραφετε is used when there is more than one person.

ὁ γοριλλος γραφει.
γραφω
The Gorilla writes.
English words: graphite; graffiti

ὁ γοριλλος σκοπει.
σκοπω
The Gorilla looks.
English words:
microscope; telescope

ὁ γοριλλος ἀριθμει.
ἀριθμω
The Gorilla counts.
English word: arithmetic

Greek Around You 7 Science 2

Physics is the study of matter and energy. **Energy** (ἐνεργεια — 'activity') exists in a number of forms, such as kinetic energy. κινησις means motion, so **kinetic** energy is the energy an object possesses owing to its motion. **Thermal** energy is in part kinetic energy, because when something is heated (θερμος — 'heat') its atoms move more quickly. **Electromagnetic** energy is connected with electrical or magnetic actions. **Electrical** takes its name from ἠλεκτρον, or amber, which becomes electrically charged when rubbed with some substances (such as fur). **Magnets** derive their name from Μαγνησια, an area in northern Greece where magnetised ore was found.

Atoms are the building-blocks of matter and contain **protons** (or positively-charged particles), **electrons** (or negatively-charged particles) and neutrons (neither positive nor negative). πρωτον (or 'first') and ἠλεκτρον ('amber') both come from Greek, but neutron comes from Latin. The original meaning of **atom** is 'uncut'. (ἀ– 'without', τομος — 'a cut'). This is because the Greek scientist Democritus, who was the first to suggest the existence of the atom, did not have the equipment to discover the still smaller particles which make up an atom.

Can you work out what terms come from the following?
γαλαξιας, πλανητης, δυναμικος, ἀτμος + σφαιρα

Answers: galaxy, planet, dynamics (the study of forces/motion), atmosphere ('vapour-sphere')

Although the term chemistry comes from Arabic, many names of chemical elements come from Greek. Sometimes these names reflect their colour. **Chlorine** is a greenish gas and the Greek χλωρος means 'green', while **iodine** takes its name from ἰον, or 'violet'. **Helium** was first detected during a solar eclipse and was therefore named after the sun (ἥλιος). **Neon** (νεον — 'new') took its name from the fact that it was a new discovery, while **hydrogen** is derived from two Greek words—ὑδωρ ('water') and γενεσις ('source'). This is because hydrogen forms water when combined with oxygen. Other names reflect less pleasant aspects. βρωμος means 'stink' and thus was a very appropriate name for **bromine**, which has a foul smell.

Biology also uses Greek terms. When a **chrysalis** (χρυσαλλις) changes into a butterfly, this is called **metamorphosis**, because it is changing its shape (μεταμορφοω — 'I transform'). **Chromosomes** (χρωμα — 'colour', σωμα — 'body') are made up of DNA. The name arose because the structures are easily stained with dyes. Chromosomes also contain **genes** (from γενεα—'race').

Some Greek words look like English ones, but have a different meaning. For example, το μηλον = apple (not melon!).

ὁ γοριλλος κρυπτει το μηλον.

The Gorilla hides the apple.

English words: <u>crypt</u>ic

ὁ γοριλλος βαλλει το μηλον.

The Gorilla throws the apple.

English word: ballistic

ὁ γοριλλος βαλλει τας σφαιρας.

The Gorilla throws the balls.

English word: <u>sphere</u>

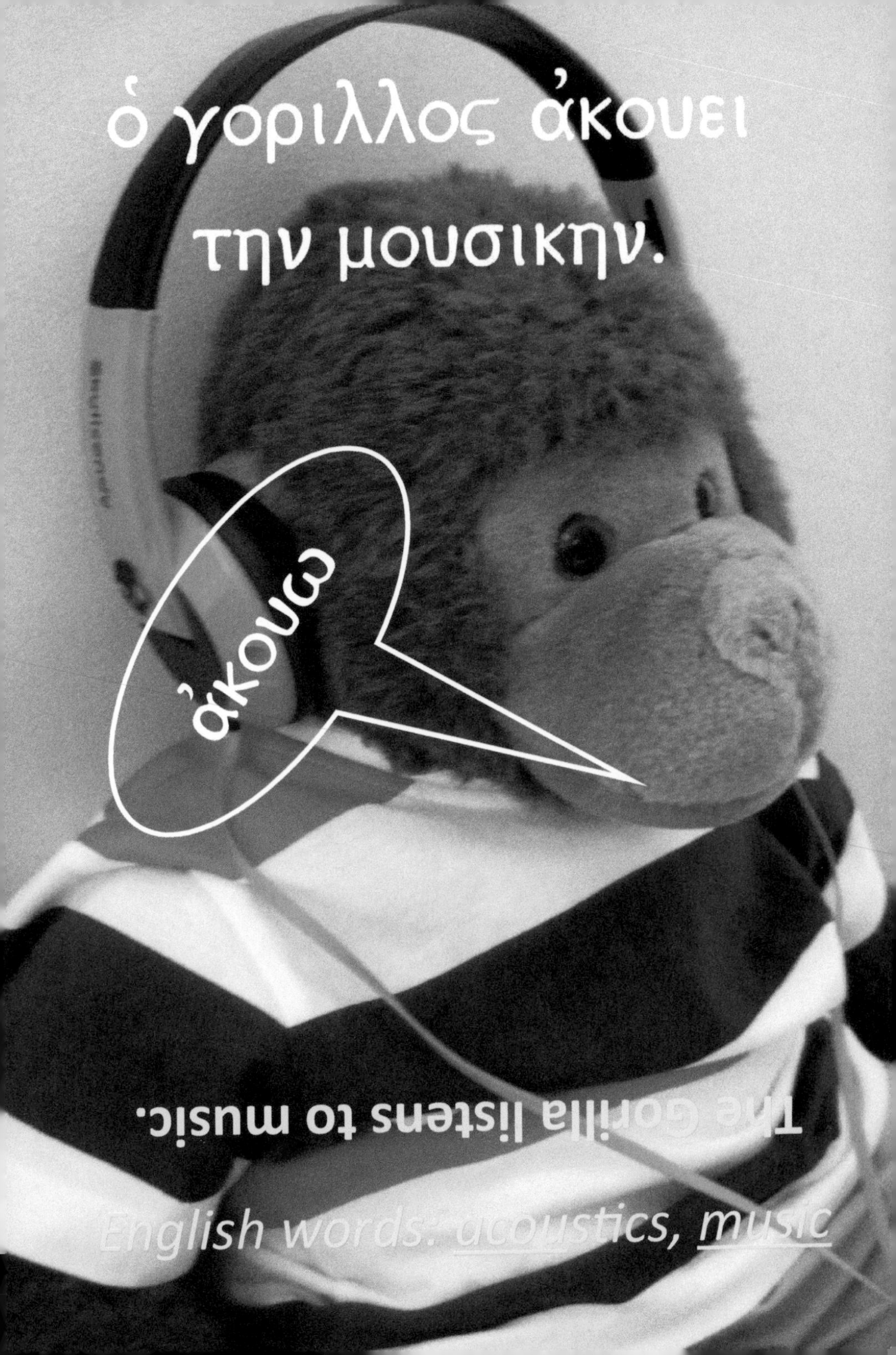
ὁ γοριλλος ἀκουει
την μουσικην.
ἀκουω
The Gorilla listens to music.
English words: acoustics, music

Drama

The Greeks invented δραμα and were the first to build theatres (θεατρον). As there was no modern system (συστημα) of microphones (μικρος— 'small', φωνη — 'voice') to project sound, the Greeks build theatres in a bowl shape to ensure the best possible acoustics (from ἀκουω —'I hear'). Different sorts of plays were put on, including comedies (κωμωδια) and tragedies (τραγῳδια). Since women were not allowed to act on stage, men played both male and female characters (χαρακτηρ). The fact that actors wore masks made this easier. There was also a chorus (χορος) of twelve or fifteen men.

The chorus sang odes (ᾠδη). These were long poems (ποιημα) which often referred to events in mythology (μυθολογια). The chorus also often sang the epilogue (ἐπιλογος), or end of the play. The prologue (προλογος) which opened the play might be spoken by either the main characters or the chorus. However, any dialogue (διαλογος) or conversation either took place between main characters or between main characters and the chorus. A monologue (μονολογος) was a speech spoken by one main character.

Words which end in –logue in English are compounds of λογος —'word' or 'speech'. The Greeks did not have newspapers or printed books, so most news and ideas were spread through discussion. The meanings of the compound words in the previous paragraph make sense when you know that μυθος means 'story', ἐπι means 'in addition', προ means 'before', δια means 'between' and μονος means 'alone'.

Plays were put on during festivals and the best won prizes. The Greek for 'judge' is **κριτης** and this gives us the English word '**critic**'. A theatre critic is someone who reviews plays and says whether they are good or bad. We also get other words from Greek. Thespis (**Θεσπις**) was supposed to be the first person ever to be an actor, so modern actors are sometimes referred to as **thespians** (or **thesps** for short). A **melodrama** is a sensational play and the word is a compound of **δραμα** and **μελος** or 'song'. (**μελος** also gives us the English word '**melody**'.) Finally, **lyrics** (or the words of a song) come from the Greek **λυρικος**, which literally means 'singing accompanied by a lyre' (or small harp).

Can you recognise these terms? The second row is harder!

προγραμμα κινημα παντομιμος ἀμφιθεατρον
σκηνη μονοτονος ἡρως μιμος παρῳδια

Answers: programme

cinema — literally 'movement' (hence why films are called 'movies', or 'motion-pictures')

pantomime — from παν ('all'), μιμος ('mimic', 'imitator')

amphitheatre — from ἀμφι ('on both sides', or 'around') and θεατρον

scene — originally, the stage on which actors performed

monotone — speaking in an unvaried pitch; from μονος ('alone') and τονος ('pitch').

hero

mime — from μιμος ('mimic', 'imitator')

parody — a mimicry of an original; from παρα ('beside') and ῳδη ('ode', 'song') ὁ γοριλλος παυει την μηχανην.

The Gorilla stops the machine.

English words: <u>pau</u>se; <u>mach</u>ine

ὁ γοριλλος μετρει.
μετρω
The Gorilla measures.
English words: metric; metre

ὁ γοριλλος γλυφει.
γλυφω
The Gorilla carves.
English word: hiero<u>glyph</u>

English words: <u>Bibl</u>e; <u>bibl</u>iography (= list of books)

History is the study of what happened in the past and comes from the Greek word ἱστορια, or 'enquiry'. Lots of words relating to history come from Greek. For example, an epoch (ἐποχη) is a period (περιοδος) of time and historical periods are often arranged chronologically (from χρονος — 'time' and λογος — 'word'). The Stone Age is divided into the Palaeolithic and Neolithic epochs. Palaeolithic comes from παλαιος ('old') and λιθος ('stone') and refers to the earlier part of the Stone Age. Neolithic refers to the later Stone Age and is derived from νεος ('new') and λιθος. Similarly, the middle Stone Age is called the Mesolithic period because μεσος means 'middle'.

ἀρχαιος means 'ancient' and gives us archaeology, or the study of ancient societies. Egyptology (from Αἰγυπτος — Egypt) includes the study of ancient Egyptian texts. Since many of the texts were found in tombs, early archaeologists assumed that the writing system was sacred and so called the letter forms hieroglyphs, from ἱερος ('sacred') and γλυφω ('I carve').

Historians also write biographies of rulers (βιος — 'life'; γραφω — 'I write'). A sequence of rulers from the same family is a dynasty (from δυναστης — 'ruler'). Some rulers may rule ruthlessly and are then called despots (δεσποτης means 'master') or tyrants (τυραννος). However, to begin with, 'tyrant' did not imply anything negative in Greek — only that the men were not hereditary monarchs.

Politics is the study of government and comes from the Greek for a city — **πολις**. The Greeks were very politically aware and devised terms for practically every sort of state. (For example, **θαλασσα** means 'sea', so a sea-power is a **thalassocracy**!) Many of these terms end in –**archy** or –**cracy**. This is because both **ἀρχη** and **κρατος** mean 'power'. **Can you link up the English and Greek words to work out who has power in the following states?**

Monarchy	δημος - the people	a few people
Plutocracy	θεος - god	everyone
Democracy	ἀριστος - the best	one ruler; a king
Oligarchy	αὐτος - self	wealthy people
Anarchy	μονος - alone	absolute government
Aristocracy	ὀλιγος - few	nobody; without rule
Theocracy	πλουτος - wealth	nobles
Autocracy	ἀν - without	priests

We also get names of people associated with each sort of power. For example, an **autocrat** is an absolute ruler, while a **democrat** wants everyone to share in power, and an **oligarch** shares power with only a few others.

Answers:

Monarchy	μονος - alone	one ruler; a king
Plutocracy	πλουτος - wealth	wealthy people
Democracy	δημος - the people	everyone
Oligarchy	ὀλιγος - few	a few people
Anarchy	ἀν - without	nobody; without rule
Aristocracy	ἀριστος - the best	nobles
Theocracy	θεος - god	priests
Autocracy	αὐτος - self	absolute government

ὁ γοριλλος ἐστιν ἀθλητης.
ἀθλητης εἰμι
The Gorilla is an athlete.
English words: athletics, athletic

ὁ γοριλλος ἐστιν ἀκροβατης.
ἀκροβατης εἰμι
The Gorilla is an acrobat.
English word: acrobatics

Although the Greeks were very keen on intellectual matters (such as literature or music), they also considered **physical** (φυσικος— 'natural') education to be very important. This was partly because it was important for their male citizens to be fit to fight in wars. It was only in **Sparta** (Σπαρτη) that girls and women had physical training, which was meant to ensure that they bred healthy, strong children!

Owing to this interest in sport, there were lots of athletic competitions in the ancient Greek world, the most famous of which were the **Olympics**, named after Ὀλυμπια, where the games took place. However, there were three other **panhellenic** or all-Greek games (παν — 'all'; Ἑλληνικος— 'Greek'). These were the **Isthmian** Games, which took place at the ἰσθμος of Corinth, the **Nemean** Games, which took place at Νεμεα and the **Pythian** Games (Πυθια) which took place at **Delphi** (Δελφοι). The Pythian Games were named in honour of the god **Apollo** (Ἀπολλων), one of whose names was Πυθιος (**Pythios**) because he had killed a monstrous **python** (Πυθων) which lurked in Delphi.

We still use many Greek terms today. **Can you recognise the following?**

ἀθλητης	γυμναστικη	δισκος	σταδιον
γυμνασιον	Μαραθων	περιμετρον	ἀκροβατης

Answers: athlete, gymnastics (so-called because athletes trained naked—γυμνος), discus, stadium, gymnasium, Marathon, perimeter (the original meaning is 'circumference' - from περι—'around', μετρον—'measure'), acrobat

Obviously, over time sport has changed considerably. However, many terms for new events or settings are derived from Greek. For example, cycling events (from κυκλος — 'circle') take place in a velodrome. The Greeks did not have either cycles or velodromes, but the '-drome' part of the word comes from δρομος, 'a track'. (The velo- part comes from the French for a bicycle). A ποδιον originally meant the foot of a vase, but has come to mean the podium on which victors stand. Even some companies have turned to Greek for an inspiration for their name — Nike takes its name for the Greek for victory (νικη).

Sometimes, people try to cheat in sport. One common way is when cheats use anabolic steroids to improve their performance. Anabolic steroid is a shorthand for 'anabolic androgenic steroids' and the whole phrase means 'steroids which throw up male characteristics'. This is because ἀναβολη means 'that which is thrown up' and androgenic comes from ἀνηρ — 'man' and γενεσις— 'sort', 'origin'. (Steroid comes from στερρος— 'solid'). However, most athletes prefer to develop their physique (from φυσικος —'produced by nature', 'natural') and technique (from τεχνη — 'skill') through exercise and diet (διαιτα— 'way of living').

If you are told the basic meaning of a verb, you can work out the meaning of a sentence even if the verb does not have an obvious English derivation (a word which comes from it). For example, πεσσω means ‘I cook’ and ἀγω means ‘I lead’. On the next page, φιλω means ’I love’ and καθευδω means ’I sleep’

The Gorilla cooks.

ὁ γοριλλος ἀγει τους φιλους.

The Gorilla leads his friends.

ὁ γοριλλος φιλει τα ἀνθεμα.
φιλω
The Gorilla loves flowers.
English word: chrysanthemum

ὁ γοριλλος και ὁ φιλος καθευδουσιν.

The Gorilla and his friend sleep.

As you saw, the Gorilla loves flowers! Lots of flowers take their name from Greek. This is partly because some of these plants grow in Greece, but also because scientists often use Greek or Latin to provide a botanical name for a plant. Indeed, the word **botany** (the study of plants) comes from the Greek **βοτανη**, which means 'pasture' or 'grass'. Moreover, some of the terms for parts of plants come from Greek. **Can you work out the following (and the name of the plant)?**

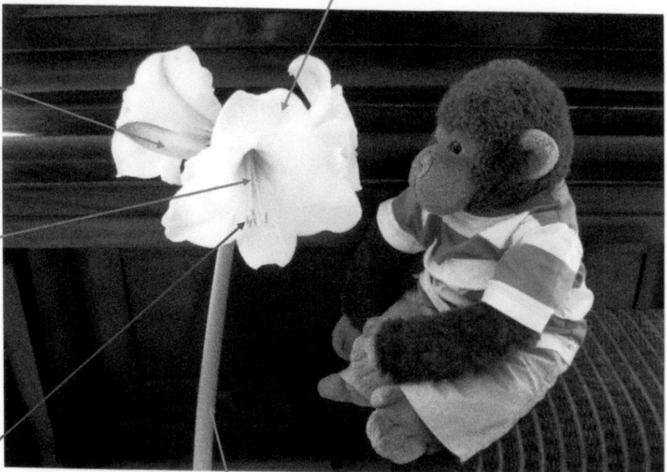

ἀνθηρα - the tip of the στημων. Insects get pollen here.

Answers: The plant is an amaryllis
petal
calyx—outer covering of the flower
stamen—the male reproductive organ of a flower
anther— tip of the stamen
chlorophyll—what gives green parts of a plant their colour (Χλωρος = green, φυλλον = a leaf)

Can you recognise the following flowers? Note that some names are spelled **–ιον** in Greek, but turn into **–ium** in English (this is because the name has come via Latin). For example, a **γερανιον** in Greek becomes a **geranium** in English.

κροκος

χρυσανθεμον

ναρκισσος

ῥοδον

πολυανθος

ὀρχις

ὑακινθος

κυκλαμινος

ῥοδοδενδρον

ἰρις

κληματις

Answers: crocus; chrysanthemum — literally 'golden-flower' (Χρυσος = golden, ἀνθεμον = flower); narcissus; rose; polyanthus — literally 'many-flower' (πολυ = many, ἀνθος = flower); orchid; hyacinth; cyclamen; rhododendron — literally 'rose-tree' (ῥοδον = rose, δενδρον = tree); iris; clematis

Mini-dictionary

ἐστι /ἐστιν	is
μικρος	small
θερμος	hot
φιλιος	friendly
μαθητης	student
κριτης	judge
μυσικος	musical
σοφος	wise
ἀρχαιολογος	archaeologist
τεχνικος	artistic
ἀρχιτεκτων	architect
στρατιωτης	soldier
ποιητης	poet
ναυτης	sailor
ἀνδρειος	brave
ἐχει	has
δωρον	gift
βασιλευς	king
καλος	handsome
ἐν	in
γη	ground, land
οἰκια	house
Μουσειον	museum
ὑπο	under

ἡλιῳ	sun
πανθηρ	panther
ὀρνιθες	birds
παρδαλις	leopard
εἰσι /εἰσιν	are
φιλος	friend
γραφει	writes
σκοπει	looks
ἀριθμει	counts
κρυπτει	hides
μηλον	apple

βαλλει	throws
σφαιρας	balls
ἀκουω	listens, hears
μουσικην	music
παυει	stops
μηχανην	machine
μετρει	measures
γλυφει	carves
ἐχει	has
βιβλον	book
ἀθλητης	athlete
ἀκροβατης	acrobat
πεσσει	cooks
ἀγει	leads
φιλους	friends
φιλει	loves
ἀνθεμα	flowers
καθευδει	sleeps

HOW VERBS WORK

A verb is a doing word. In Greek, the start of a verb shows the basic meaning and the endings show who is doing the action.

For example, γραφω means 'I write'. The γραφ– bit gives the basic meaning 'write', while the –ω ending shows that 'I' am doing the writing.

Similarly, γραφει means 'he' or 'she' writes. The γραφ– bit gives the basic meaning 'write', while the –ει ending shows that 'he' or 'she' is doing the writing.

The different forms of the verb are:

γραφω	I write	γραφομεν	we write
γραφεις	you write	γραφετε	you write
γραφει	he or she writes	γραφουσι	they write

The verb 'to be' is less regular:

εἰμι	I am	ἐσμεν = we are
εἰ	you are	ἐστε = you are
ἐστι or ἐστιν	he is (or 'is')	εἰσι or εἰσιν = they are (or 'are')

The two forms of 'you'. One (like γραφεις) is used when there is only one person involved. The other (like γραφετε) is used when there is more than one person.

THE ALPHABET

Greek	name	English equivalent
α, Α	alpha	a, A
β, Β	beta	b, B
γ, Γ	gamma	g, G
δ, Δ	delta	d, D
ε, Ε	epsilon	e, E (short e, as in get)
ζ, Ζ	zeta	z, Z
η, Η	eta	e, E (long e, as in hair)
θ, Θ	theta	th, Th
ι, Ι	iota	i, I
κ, Κ	kappa	k, K
λ, Λ	lambda	l, L
μ, Μ	mu	m, M
ν, Ν	nu	n, N
ξ, Ξ	xi	x, X
ο, Ο	omicron	o, O (short o, as in got)
π, Π	pi	p, P
ρ, Ρ	rho	r, R
σ, ς, Σ	sigma	s, S (σ in middle of words, ς at end)
τ, Τ	tau	t, T
υ, Υ	upsilon	u, U
φ, Φ	phi	ph, Ph
χ, Χ	chi	ch, Ch (as in loch)
ψ, Ψ	psi	ps, Ps
ω, Ω	omega	o, O (long o, as in oar)

‘ = an h sound before a letter e.g. ἡλιος = helios (sun)

’ = no h sound before a letter e.g. ἐστι = esti (he is)

The Gorilla would like to thank: Dr Susanna Phillippo; Professor M. Schofield; Dr J. Taylor; Professor C. Pelling; James Renshaw; MBF; Dr P.G. Wright; Dr M.R. Wright; TB and RN; Alex and Diana Hayes; Sarah and Lucy; Dorothy Anderson; Bob Bass; Arbeia Roman Fort (p17); Vindolanda Trust (pp22, 30); Beth Russell Needlepoint (p36); Trinity College, Cambridge (p6); Wycombe Abbey; St Mary's, Ascot, particularly AMW's 2012–13 Year 11 Latin and Greek sets and Year 10 Latin set.

The author would like to thank all of the above and especially the Great Ape himself, who patiently endured the trials and tribulations of photo shoots.

Printed and bound by CPI Group (UK) Ltd, Croydon CR0 4YY

First published 2013

Designed and typeset by Anne Wright
Files prepared for printing by Ruth Thomas, www.rhthomeditorial.weebly.com

ISBN: 978 0 9926200 0 4